From El Salvador to Los Angeles, this deeply-moving book works to "occupy the dark" not with coercive force but through empathy, compassion, and witness. "Be mindful," "Take note," "Pay attention"—a powerful rhetoric of recognition courses through *S is For*, coupled with extraordinary lyric grace: "Lament/ happens so gradually/ no one ever notices the dust/ settling on the lemon trees." There's a lot of socially engaged poetry being written in America right now, and none of it is more powerful, purposeful, intimate or important than these poems by William Archila.

—Campbell McGrath

A poetic voyage that explores the ethics of memory from the hell of dictatorships to the splendid fortitude of the soul, William Archila has given us a work of great splendor and fortitude. A memorable reading.

—Marjorie Agosin

S is For

Poems

WILLIAM ARCHILA

BLACK LAWRENCE PRESS

Black Lawrence Press

Executive Editor: Diane Goettel
Book Cover and Interior Design: Zoe Norvell
Front Cover Artwork: A Way of Flying" by Francisco Goya

Published 2025 by Black Lawrence Press.
Printed in the United States.

Table of Contents

I am a man of substance, of flesh and bone, fiber and liquids-
and I might even be said to possess a mind. I am invisible,
understand, simply because people refuse to see me.

—Ralph Ellison, *Invisible Man*

[He] never made a lot of money. His name was never in the
paper...but he's a human being, and a terrible thing is happening
to him. So attention must be paid. He's not to be allowed to fall
into his grave like an old dog.

—Henry Miller, *Death of a Salesman*

La cabeza inventa un terruño que sólo yo conozco

—Roberto Armijo

And etcetera, etcetera, etcetera.
My etcetera country

—Claribel Alegria

Posting. Boasting. Eighty rounds from an officer. Burning.
Looting. The life of a minor always leads to a line of corpses.
Segregated schools, segregated hoods. Not enough money
in the bank for representation. For a voice. For a commercial.

Be mindful of minutemen, pilgrims, unidentified men unhinged
who donate money to old white men in suits executing laws.
Take note of drug-trafficking with the pistol of a teenage assassin.
Pay attention to his invisible hoodie stitched to his head.

Try to count backwards. Try days swollen & cracked backwards.
Try School of the Americas in Georgia. Try Atlácatl Battalion.
Try city hall. Try the coroner's log. Be vigilant of the government
as the ghost of God, including Michelangelo & his cadavers.

Also taking care of other people's babies, crybabies & shitloaders.
Wiping. Mopping. What else? What else makes you disappear?

BEYOND BRUEGEL'S SHORE

Somewhere in Nicaragua or Guatemala
it doesn't matter, his wings ache
from so much wax, so much discord
in his father's voice, how once
he fled the wards of the state
through air & sky; so simple
& so exact he fell from the clouds
yet no one cared; not the hospitals
not the impoverished nor the imprisoned.
For years, the diagrams of his nerves
branched in confinement. And yet
he has begun a new life
one of labor, of wife & child
his house asleep by the shore, a few
cattle battering the fattening ground.
But something has begun to crack
that dizzy spell of mist, that depth
sweeping over him, blaring in the dark
that thick, rough side of the sea.
This time he set up his gear
because he had to, with no choice
but to curse the coming waters.
This time he swooped so low
he could finger the waves, dropped so low
the foam soaked his hull of feathers.
It's just as well, he banished

it all to the barn. The plowing goes on
but today in Central America it does matter
another boy fell from the sky, chicken fluff & all
body tangled, indeed body tangled.
And there was no one around.

CENTRAL AMERICAN BOYS

They   the product they pack

    chronic culprit in love with bullets

        plucked like stars.

They   the glance at each other

    crossing the street, the way they know

        their fathers will never come back.

    Profanity, yes. Illiterate, ill-nourished

        most of them, most definitely. In addition

            the brilliant genesis of Odysseus.

They   small ghosts

    like pale plates of water abandoned

        under the brush. It might as well

be a jar of snares   mosquitoes

damn mosquitoes to get rid of

draining the blood for eggs.

They

        the memory of a stowaway

        hitting the ground again

        & again.

NORTHERN TRIANGLE DISSECTED

*Central America is a region of great importance to the
United States. And it is so close: San Salvador is closer to
Houston, Texas than Houston is to Washington, DC.*
– Ronald Reagan

País mío no existes. – Roque Dalton

#1

I must tell you the truth.
Sometimes I want nothing more
than the continent capsized; north
down there, south the top of the head
between you & me not a line
no scrape of rust clogging
the mind. Who's to say? Me
the dark design
                              of a collarbone.
Of a country & without a country.

It's hard to grasp the God-awful hunger
of those who don't see it, don't need it
rather bury it, the body
as the greatest instrument.

                    How small
the countries of our bodies.

#2

You come in like the Spanish flu
ravaging the blossoms' water supply.

Our rejection out of old rage begins
as if a Mayflower found itself

unanchored, a searing crucible
with no return. The story you claim

disturbing & enchanting.
Such a rotten thing. May you find

your whole way back
through the black dogs of gunfire

harken back to the sounds
of your native flowers. Chances are

if you fall, you'll disappear
or pass. Yet like a hawk

I will coin myself vigilant, dig you out
before your weeds, blackening

spawn your way of life. Our bodies
settled here first.

#3

If there's no body left, there's no crime
no court case, so bury the filthy bastard.
Don't fuss about it. It's just a quick blow
down he goes. You see the brains

unclogged like leafed rainwater
in the gutters. My bag. My haunt of flies.
Thinking of nothing will make nothing
happen, so nothing will
do precisely. Nothing.

#4

Here by the northern peak, they cut
the chine of another country, blue
pre-dawn, darkened highway.

Another checkpoint, & whatever
they carry speaks of cadavers—
all those vanishings
by whatever means necessary—

not our Eden, crushed forest
of mangled trees & brush
brushed aside, not you asleep
as if beneath the fields.

#5

The sun foaming with too much hissing
mirrors the indifference of scrub
mountain gut, scorching haze
as they snake through thorns
vanish through trees &, on the rocks
settle like dust.
                              With light sleep
with music and argot unheard
moving on instinct, they
puncture their countries, not knowing
what it means, & why would they
after all they were taught to eat
everything, including the roaches.

#6

I'm not sorry, not at all
for the highway I've taken
rapacious, moldering
hollow husk of a highway.
My destination deemed
perfect, where everybody
collides, so says the law
whether I'm a criminal
or not, the math doesn't add up
to exchange a few nothings

for a heaven I've never seen
always heard of, right?
No maps nor numbers
no possible word written
or spoken to keep you
from thinking I'm putting
a dent in your narrow
pockets. This is how
I do it, while the bald
mountains arch their backs
darkness coming in fast
something to chew
while my body rots.

#7

A match light like a bold
faded gold leaf falling
in a painting. There
in the back streets
failing once again to form
a lucid thought. That's
the only way to carry out
before you tread, watch
the landscape change.
How else is it possible
to obliterate one's country.
Not completely, just enough
to feel dead or almost

in the flesh. How once
you rose on the other side
only to hear a shout babble
a language you didn't know
words you knew lost their worth.
The roof of your mouth ossified
tongue only the space it used
to take. At ease with the dark.
At ease with your reflection
blurred in public restrooms.
That's the only way to go.
No grasp of what it's like
to leave without wanting
to come back, to leave
without all you know, all you are
as if the doctor has cut a wedge
out of the brain. It's getting here
that makes it difficult to ignore
the flicker of a thought
discarded like a cigarette.

#8

You heard this before
country of volcanoes
& lakes, country of
I break your ass, I pry
you open with rocks

out of ravines, out of
tangled hills of my mind
without a guide on all
fours I walk. Illegitimate
country of legs & arms
in a way a rosary I have
nothing to say, nothing
to add, except I'm ashamed
I lost it. Country of piece-
of-shit Coca-Cola, torso
& head, I piece you
like a forsaken blanket
over the shoulder, how
does one forget such
weight, how does leaving
mean much more than
returning. I want to say
a voice well-crafted
& resurrected said
you don't exist. I think
I know what he meant.
Country that is no
country, crevice so far
and so close to —
here is the thing. Maybe
I'll never get there, but
when I do, no doubt
I'll look back, thinking
someone is following.

ADVICE TO A MIGRANT COLLECTING
DEAD THINGS

Leave them. Only
   heavy clothing
      in a knapsack.
Don't talk
   nor make a sound. We
      don't want anyone
to hear our lips utter God
   be wicked or God be askew
      with you. From now on
all roots & runners
   will contain a silence
      you've never known
a life grown all of its
   own. Don't look back
      to the slightest point
of light. Not much
   can be done until
      we get out. Leave it.
The smallest
   possibility to pull
      your country
leave it. It's pitch
   December, its abridged
      tremor, saying
here's your state
   broken by rain, here's

how puddles
carve a pothole
    into your head
        how night dented
buckling over
    the highway, abandoned
        by some wrecked
lanterns, dim single-bulb houses
    gone completely quiet, saying
enough, enough of you.

ALL FOOT & BONE

for my Central American students

They will tell you
I smoked weed, that I kicked

    my mother in the ribs, that I shook her loose
couldn't hold a baby or a job

  whatever it took   to incarcerate me.

Is it too much to ask
    for the footsteps still out

    in the brush. Hand over the dollars
    or drown. Brush of bones, brush of

    discarded clothes. Let me show you
when night comes   its sweet smell,

its rough earth. Follow the trail
or they'll take you for dead.

    Whether I'm a boy with a soul
    or a dog with a mind, they'll break

my stiff collar   break the whisper
    of a moth. I have no choice

but to walk it, the hours, the whole tract
to believe   in one more day

risking the thought
    of losing the only moon

in my pocket, but I can't go back now
    & I can't explain   why I cannot

    concentrate. I have so much
faith in my legs. I will scratch.

    I will dig & growl, but I will not die

like a hairy carcass.   All this to say
I am tired of the mind   falling behind.

All this to say   there's a bus
enveloped in flames.   How long

    beneath the tooth-shaped
mountains. Over the rugged road

I need a mind to sleepwalk
    to walk the desert back.

Here's how clay becomes a crime. Just like that, they're here
with a package you left behind. There's no way of flocking them
together like yardbirds in a cage. They want someone like Virgil
the length of a mind for a possible life. All you have to do is paw
the hole's bottom, exhume the tint you considered an afterthought.
All you have to do is listen to directions on how to get back.

Wee-size roosters roughly glazed, low-dollar drunks roughly cut
cops with glasses that look a lot like Pinochet, market-headed
women gathered thick together. All of them pulled from a barrow
in Ilobasco. The rub, the spine, spit shine till the body thickens
into a fistful of mud. In other words, cheaply made, two for one
specials, laid out for you to probe & handle their citizenship.

When the phone rings in the middle of night, it's not God who puts
them on hold for hours, but elevated talk that leaves them in the dark.

ALL THINGS DARK; ARGUMENT FOR
A MIGRANT

   What I'm saying is
he descends without a guide
more or less insane
                 down like a robe

lit by a match, waist-deep   in the waters
    then stalagmites rise   & stalactites fall
      only to find a translation
   he knows too well   how simple
it feels to feel strange.

What I'm saying is
stumbling back to the light
   he retraces his steps   out
   to their gilded cross   bent knee
on the shore   out to find
the shipwrecked   Spaniards.

No one deserves that entrapment
not the dealer, not the pope, not the day
   inside the body of a bag.

              No brimstone, just skillful order

getting doped   on the way delegates

rephrase the facts

something in the flak

when walls go up

the way you give up

or get off the ground

because there's a belief

like kingdom come

that you are generous
that you can make another human being   feel good.

What I mean is
it's dark in here, bottlenecked into the desert
the color of clot   of a godless god

but he's done with that, lost enough to admit

there's always something foul   that takes hold

how simple
it feels to feel strange

something uncanny
doing the dirty work.

EL MOZOTE

The only movement is the movement
of the monument. The contour
the black metal. You turn the page

& the family rises. No arch, no thistle
the town remains denuded of its residents
many years the very picture lost in the hills.

Stunning, the number of shoes
tricycles mangled. The absence
of physical grace, the cadence

of a well-tuned body. The photograph
leads you to coarse lines
crooked along weathered grains

of a wooden tablet, probably painted
by a carpenter or wood cutter
loops around the bowl whitewashed

the color of clarity. Anacleta
Amílcar, Macario. Names branded
for a testament of wood & rock.

The morning the deer roamed
the thick of the woods, panels
of the sky capsized; the stare innocent

the cut unclean. The bar, the stem
the height. Cayetano, Candelaria
Concepcion built like a house.

The sacristy burned
the way wood transforms to fire.
Out of rubble, fire. Femurs

afire. Like Milton's Late Massacre
they're outdated to the jury, robbed
of their own eyes, yet everything

is archived in the clouds. Doroteo
Filomena, Facundo. Each name
a chamber, a chapel, fragment of a line

like an off-rhyme or a shotgun blast. The bending
& brushing. Insects, vessel-like roots
reaching for foliage; Zoila, Clicerio

Olayo. Lines of a child. A minefield.

LETTERS & NUMBERS

Everyone knows why they're dying
to the slayings everyone agrees
though some disagree at the rate
they disappear - downtown
two to three, another in the middle
of nowhere. It's in the countryside
so why mention it. So says the anchorman
when no one's watching. The guards
grind their tools with iron fingers
which do not work at first, so
ingeniously the president designs
the iron fist. Some street vendors
want a truce cut clean. Go ask
the store owner, go ask the lady
at the corner palming pupusas
but the Jesuits say that's a box
too difficult to unlock if the keys
are kept too long in the wrong hands.
Yesterday a cutthroat carved a copper
who carved a cutthroat, 224 wounds
for the smallest of spoils. My cousin
saw the whole thing this morning
the young man laid out for the flies
like a banquet. All to say his wife & child
listen to the figures of the rain take shape
how the frogs sing their round
out of rocks. All their lives branded

like a block stamp on their foreheads.
It's obvious there's no consolation
in a little republic like this one
with its little stains of blood
its clay torsos running amok.
Come morning everyone wakes up
to a thousand daggers, everyone robbed
& the bus assaulted, but for this child
who carries the unclaimed calligraphy
of her father's name on her chest
come evening, the wet smudge of the stars
no one will be killed with the aid
of a gun or a knife. Not one.

SPANISH LOVE SONGS

You must've been a boy when you were here
listening to the rain collect

its precise execution, each verse composed
an anthophilous anthology of words—

the same star-cross'd lovers, the same
entanglement of a thousand greens

about to unfurl. Sometimes the fanfare
of violins takes you to a trench

where the earth is shoveled
to the depth of the death squads.

You loved none & none loved you back
but you were there, wound tight like a rope

in love with the idea of a common girl.
Each couple plastered at the park implied

some incomprehensible transaction, some
affair subject to drama, ripe

with lust & a little house by the hillside
where the kids can run and play.

You were warned not to sleep
one more night in the moonlit lung

of your house, else you'd be dragged out
& drowned. The past is past

says the singer, but here you are
far removed from that trench. And yet

the radio keeps skylarking song
after sweaty song, where they're condemned

to fall, to lie, to reconcile, all of it
in a single refrain, all those bodies consumed

nightly by the impassive sound of a cricket.

OUR MOUTHS, LAURELS & LILIES

in the slump of the street   they shot him
necklace down   cologne & golden watch

down with his cargo bike   the bullet's nose
broke the sun's sweat   the shot's echo

hit the back of our heads   like ants
we all scattered to the ground   to the kitchen

floor   down the gutter   our teeth nailed
our teeth black   against the graveyard

under the bed   hide under the bed
my cousin said   they shot him   & now

he has rocks in his mouth   laurels & lilies
round his face   the wind's moisture

against his tiny window   a fragment
of darkness   down he went   quietly down

the thud's echo   hit the back of our heads
all our pores on the casket   we touched

the periphery of the earth   we lit matches
spread like mist   neolithic over the streets

SATURN'S COUNTRY

S for salt, for
spoiling crops. S
for worse or
no choice other
than exodus or
a territorial discourse.
S for stretched out
in a morgue, plastic
bags like garbage
you discard. S
for ES which is S
which is señor of a
thousand choruses.
S for stinking hog
onions, frenetic
maggots laying
their baggage. S
for still you're flesh
meat butchered, bootlegged
in the marketplace. S
some might say
you're gas sloshed
from a tank. Others
that first blue
God doused
on a tarp, hated it
& left it to rot, or

you're that sound
he loved so much
smaller than a
cricket song.
S for scalp, for the soiled
search of your god. S
for complete
utter darkness. S
for success
out of the carcass.
S for sloth, for
sickle, for a solar system
beyond sable
incarceration.
S for savior, for
scavengers & sculptors
you throw out
of the temple. S
for so much white-
noise pressure
even the cardinal
won't canonize you.
No, not that bird, not
that pontiff, nor your
arsenal. S for still
to this day in your
belly, in the dive
of your mouth.

SALVIS PLAY SHAKESPEARE

Play it in the fifth, & only in the fifth, like it's the last dusk
for such a life. Play it to restore the incomplete vault of names
at church. Play it if you must go & follow those who follow
the procession. If someone's gun must guffaw, let it go.
Whoever wails the loudest will get their treatment. Drag
the procession. Nothing black or baroque, even the bones
of a mother must be kept away. It's possible, but if you must
you must let her choke. This is not the orchestration of sobs
for display. This is feeling the weight of the box, backs going numb
fingers crooked around the corners of the boy, that rugged suitcase
unhinged & gutted, that bastard hammered to the mountains.
The digging should be rough, homegrown, shoulders & sweat
tearing at the gravel. No bulldozer or hired hands. No rose
no toss. So, get out the smokes. Take off your shoes, get a shovel.

VARIATIONS ON MOTHERWELL'S
ELEGIES TO THE SPANISH REPUBLIC

I like the black & white. I like
the mirage they create. I like
planes. I like stray dogs
who never forget where I come from.

I like when my mother flings
her bridal sheets over the clothesline

sweeping the canvas with a stroke
so subtle, daylight

    blots out the night
& every flying thing breathes

its vertical breathing
every breathing thing wakes

to the impalpable span
    of another dark season.

      ~

I remember the morning serenity
shattered the chandelier

a council of crows
clouded the twisted torso

& over the lake
the composition of a young man
like a mist breaks the waters.

~

What makes the light so white
the erasure of a town

comes to mind. No line
        of trees left behind

by a cluster of bombs saying
        here's God, or the lack of it

trapped in a throat
                        so narrow

the whole cranium cracks
its own geometry.

~

Even evening gores
its horns into the coppice

of blackbirds, the tone
    so precise the clatter

of a building disperses
& is down like a monument.

Of those countries, the volcanoes
      remain the best.

    ~

What makes night fall out
like a tent? Catch the rain?

   Take the shape of a wave
as if a wave could roof a mind?

What compost? What composition?
   What clarity can I come to?

    ~

Everyone knows the bull
stumbling like a medieval god

   wrecks the fabric
of the furrow. The desolate plow

whispers to the ground
   & the splendid soil

feeds the gospel of the body.

~

In a road like this, one might understand
the periphery of trees

how they dot the skyline
how the mind leaves out

the gray, how it begins
to sag, to tear, cracked feet, cracked

hands come forth
to imply nothing's fixed.

~

I like balconies, I like clocks.

I like Nicaragua
& the songs
of my boyhood.

I remember mostly black & white.

ID documents from a log
snapshots, mugshots against the wall

the partial arc of an official stamp
still visible, but zoom closer
          & the low resolution diffuses

every dot an organic
stroke of grace   so light & dark

strong enough to bruise the sky

...Araceli De Paz...Carlos Armando Guillen...Giovani
Dubon...Andres Duke Castro...

Demetria Rosales...Rosa Henrique Otero...Isabel Rodriguez...
Baltazar Antolin Flores

...Sandra Yanira Hernandez...Luis Mejia Sorano...Elsy Victoria
Martinez...Orlando

Quiñonez...Dora Calero...Arsenio Gomez Cardenal...Maria
Guadalupe Morales...

Ruben Gutierrez...Reina Maribel Ponce...Jose Manuel
Garcia...Idalia Lopez Salazar...

Honorilo Lobo...Elena Juachin...Nicolas Escobar...Silvia
Beatriz Hernandez Artiga...

ON INVISIBILITY

Only the dark knows
you exist. Only

shovels & brooms know
the dirt grows thicker

moist after bodies
have built colonies

of habits, whether
deep in its chambers

or left alone with
roaches, I'm done with

memory. To have
a biography

to have nothing to
say & go nowhere.

                *

I'm anchored in my
suit, my bowtie &

hat, more interested
with my ghostly state

than catching the stage
of light. I'm always

astonished by the
sense of nothing that

opens itself to
deserted taverns.

*

That's too many Is
on this lonely sight.

*

In my mother's womb
was the first time I

played dead, then the curb
ditches by the lake

beneath the bed, each
time a murder of

crows watched from the wires
the rows of bodies.

*

To say how it feels
simply uttered is

an understatement.
To know between light

& complete utter
darkness is to know

when it comes about
only the stray &

the blind understand
the dead. I too wait

for someone like a
god to arrive, a

carbon copy of
a country without.

*

That's too many Is
on this lonely sight.

*

Some use a cloak or
a ring to retreat

from everything, from
God's promises to

straight-up sickness to
a kingdom, rain-streaked

cardboard housing &
all those small-time dogs.

              *

If you look close, I
don't absorb, neither

reflect light, all my
living empty, my

tongue a choir of flies
so dead it retires

but my thinking, like
a lantern, eyes &

mouth casting out bro-
ken halos of light.

              *

When the crone sweeping
the doorstep reaches

for her glasses it's
clear she can't see me.

SPIRITS

At daylight, he surrendered to the gutters'
thick cirrhosis, his trajectory

half awake, half anvil from the glass to the killing floor
I was raised in, each thin thread tethered

from the root of a nicotined tooth
to the rusted bars of the slammer. I couldn't tell you

why Felix the Cat came to mind, totally inebriated
two Xs, bubbles popping, his gait

a saint carried in a procession—Cherry Pink
& Apple Blossom White, 1955—

except that my grandfather died
with a bottle in his pocket, his Robert Mitchum

chin & pompadour distilled
from a banana republic in fire, a slow, steady

drinker, perfect fulfillment to drown out
his manhood. There's a certain kind of fix

that falters precariously
a benediction when they allege

one more drunk for the hood. He didn't matter
to the dispenser nor the riffraff crowd.

Nothing about him capsized, except his compound
of cologne & corrosion. All those rotguts.

All those bums. They didn't matter
to the nation, though they were the nation.

A lamp lit in my father's body, that tarnished brown
of the mind that taints the night & eats highways
has caked a vagrant cockroach out to nowhere
without a horse or land, without the act to hurl himself

in the present tense. He remembers none of the country
except the confidence for a cold clutch of dollars
clenched in his hands. God descends, & says nothing
despite darkness dressed in clay. Farther & farther

my father disappears farther from the piece of ground
he never wanted. This is the music I could call mine
my own fragment shining on a hill, own it the way
sleep in my head is another galaxy, another tire's grating

against the gravel, an arrival like a holy canticle
to a cathedral we never attended. At any hour, anvil black
I read with a hawk's yellow eye, the lay of the land dug out
my mouth exhausted. A highway in my father's body.

WHEN I THINK OF ALEPPO

for Zevart Bedikian (1937-2020)

I too lived a war, but I don't think
I necessarily have to like the alternative

for permanent residence. There are ways
to be cursed when a brother ends up

in a rival gang, & you must throw down
because the feud is on, the way of

Polynices and Eteocles. It's complicated
the way I associate my mother-in-law

with Aleppo, or the photo of two
Syrian boys sitting in rubble, one

torn sweater-arm over the other's
shoulder, two years older than my sons

asleep in the darkness of another siren.
I think more & more in parallels now

because there's a feeling in me
that outlives my way of thinking.

How do I articulate to the boys
stop shoveling, it's time to go.

Time to drop the front loaders,
stop shouting at each other. I think

of the Syrian boys as if my thinking
can restore their bodies. What it is

is the insignificant feeling of a span
much too short. And what would I do

if it comes taking everything sweet as dirt.
To feel all night birds flooding over the sky

to murder the smudge
of stars. Not now, not ever,

not for another barrel bomb will I
contribute to your faceless justice. This

is what makes my body hum at night.
To elevate that which is broken

bone & tendon, assembling the body
out of fragments. This is to say

I got my boys going down the slide
the way they pick their small bodies

off the grass is an accomplishment.
I can't tell you how many times

I have lied for the sake of making logic
work, believing I'm all right

that I can stomach another grave.
It's so simple, so obvious, but I go on

blind to the war, like that fool Oedipus
who concludes that *All is well.*

LAS TÍAS

They get together in the evenings
for coffee & *pan dulce*
when the weather is cool

and the white handkerchief out
for a sniff is a sign of colonial
elegance. They talk

in a tone of *hamacas*
in a hospice, medieval cathedral
in the form of a son

who can no longer reinvent
the sign of the cross. Eyeglasses
rimmed for the metal frame

of their lives in a small town. Belt
with a metal buckle to mark
the equator line around the barrel

of a gut. They come with flapping arms
around children saying, *vengan,*
sientense, vengan a comer.

Plaza pigeons are their lonely
apprentices, demanding a court case
for the death of their children.

Where are they going
in their proper sadness. Lament
happens so gradually

no one ever notices the dust
settling on the lemon trees.
Once home, nap of pears

& baby's hair. Las tías
in their lavender & moth scent
in the blue flame of their stove

who boil water & oils
who board a plane every night
& never make it back.

SESTINA

It sounds like a tía's name, the veil
of it, the transformation of it, a voice that sounds
repetitive like coffee & cigarettes, circular conversation
about pale women from Roman Catholic countries
a spinster who never got married
her dark rimmed glasses, looking nothing

like Jackie Onassis. My aunt has nothing
to say about her siestas, her snore, her veil
folded in the armoire, or the man she never married—
tall, handsome troubadour with a voice that sounds
like a Neruda love poem, winding a country
road after hours, each poem a conversation

she never answered. Erotic conversations
always the topic, though she says *it was nothing
like that. All lies.* She's such a country
girl. Hooking crochet, she has managed to veil
her heart behind the black lace, all sound
and slow fire for couples newly married.

She's no raconteuse either, unless she marries
her whiskey & coffee. Then the conversation
turns around to the man she never found sound
a hellhound consecrated to handle her vessel, nothing
sacred, just a distraction from taking the veil
to become an old maid in the country.

During the war she fled city & country
a brief trip with the darling who asked her to marry
while heavy smoke like a blanket veiled
the ground. She smokes well, but has no conversation
about her life abroad, no sigh for her troubadour, nothing
of a courtly love making all kinds of love sounds

except the single memory of the s sound
stressed heavily when he called her *sueño*. In another country
he has a wife & kids, a house by the beach. *It's nothing*
she says, while she watches the neighbors' children marry.
She's so Catholic she dresses our conversations
in private, how her faith for Christ veils

her love for her troubadour, a sound like a veil
of smoke, conversations of autumn & war in a country
where young marrieds in their newly home mean nothing.

This field of weeds & wildflowers

If I were a painter, I'd start with blue   the color field

as in Sonny Rollins' *Colossus*. As in Ruben Dario's *Azul*.
Shelve it. If this were a landscape   thick over thin

intended   or less ornate than a volcano, I'd say
blue like the midday sky or the midday heart

all the birds in Central America madcap. If I had a choice
this oil.   This water.   This lank tool I fool

in my fingers, I'd say the theatrical   blue flame
in a gas stove. Like the black & blue

on my torso, the enormity of it, the batons & asphalt
in blue uniforms.   This Vicks VapoRub jar   clad

on my grandmother's bedside   this asteroid snug fit
in a gravesite   darker than soot, darker

than the coiled look of feathered things.   Her morning walk
her morning song   down the hallway   the mud, the match

when she joined the landscape of birds.   This field
of weeds & wildflowers   let me brush

my hand over the canvas   like in a mirror   how faithful
the camphor.   Her eucalyptus. Her mint

I sniff & smear   on my nostrils. All the blood tint
this cold   blue pigment   all the ink   blue

as a painter   who wipes stained fingers   on her apron.

CHILDHOOD

When it comes, my father's presence
stands behind the weight of a country
I've lost, like I've lost him, on his way out
over the hill, flooring his decrepit wagon
exhaust pipe exhausted, which brings me
to bed, to the sleep of a sunken log
at the river's bottom, & my father in it
like some huge bear wavering through
the thickest depths, all the while, I keep
my eye on the shimmering surface of light
wishing to come up for air, but I don't
want to forsake this absent god
tired in the pale grass.
                              He's been leaving
for so long, it almost seems natural, his aimless
driving, aimless thinking. Outside, a helicopter
that may or may not allow me to continue
keeps announcing its presence
clambering out of the rain clouds.
It's so frustrating, knowing all I have to do
is turn off the light to occupy the dark.

DEAR REPUBLIC

I want to tell you every argument against disappearing
should be turned over & exposed. What matters most
is the invention of our unbearable presence. I want to live there
in the middle of its own well, a gleaming light devoted to clarity.

There must be something inside, something like oxygen
settling over the gravesites & stones, enough to climate the
     weather
fit for a ghost, my boy's umbilical cord. There's nothing here to
     change
but the mind of a block. There must be something else outside.

This is half you, half my invisibility formed. Half my struggle
to construct my ark, my family with petals curling on the dark
     day
of my birth. Only I can do it mediocrely, fail miserably, with
     fingers
wide, limbered pull out the cartography of earth. Is it my body?

Is my river a ruined narrative? Sometimes I feel haunted by the
     very
margins of my story. You can see the trace & pause in my
     walking.
Who are they, in their elegant decay, the marble souls of their
     children
bothered by my presence, in their perfect pitch & breed, still
     hungry?

CITY OF

City of ghosts. City of dead cars. City of nah to the songs
that say blah, blah, blah. Is this what I get
when my father's dead. Is this what I get when I'm lonely

in my veins. I don't feel like watching TV
or listening to the stereo set. My heart downtown
has nowhere to go except where the dead reside

suddenly the choreography of bodies sleeping
in tents by the lake, some angelenos, some illegal
what is like to shake with an ashtray's click of cigarettes.

Now tell me, doesn't the desert eat unless daylight
is winding down like a siren. Lawmakers smell of cash
because they eat cash, says my father, while I grow old

& nocturnal. Inside the eloquent darkness the blue comes out
in the dirt. I don't know what the worms do inside the earth.
I don't know why I'm more tired than a dog revised

in a graveyard, tired of american gothic gentrified
disgusted by plastic, by the gutting of carcasses
where others have gone off to praise

the four black, shiny SUVs parked in the driveway
I've deserted to the streets, deserted to odes & elegies.
It's strange to think beyond that window another exile

is probably thinking the same as me. You can find
almost anything. City of cocktails. City of cops. City of
carnations crushed & taco trucks.

CIVIL ENGINEERING

It's one of those turns when I'm up
all night watching old flicks on TV
in other words, a suit in a fedora hat
scanning the vertical lines
of a building downtown. Always
the red pulse of the neon sign
the endless drag, the endless fall
twenty floors down. Of course
it's all about the femme fatale
when a stranger arrives in town
but even a nickel-and-dime dick
won't set the city straight, even
crooks behind bars won't do the job.
How come a hard rain after ten p.m.
isn't enough? How come a flood
won't wash the scum? Call it feeble
or simple-minded. Call it arrested
development of the faculties
but the Romantic in me, the stroller
with a loaf of bread along the streets
prefers the architecture of the woods
to a dogmatic parking lot. Maybe
hand the dishwasher an ash, his chum
the hash slinger, an aspen, an elm
to the gangster, a cypress in all its
gratitude to the destitute. I know
there's no pine tall enough

to shelter the welfare system
but a boy wants a prospective family
possibly his own parents gone
one at a time to roost, even though
he doesn't care, no one believes it.
Still he wants the chapel of a backyard
where the yawning grass beckons
the congress of timber. It's possible
to build it, to give the welfare
till it kills us; the welfare
of the well-off trees, closer
to the ground's gorgeous blueprint.
More than that, every matured oak
will have the lonely corner
of a liquor store, & every window
lit like a votive will have
its own sycamore.

CINE NEGRO

Opening shot: a nocturnal get-out-of-town
glare of a cityscape. Concrete overcoat

& sprawling steel lengthens along
the electric crackle, its blood, its fevers

clad in coats darker than fog. Now
arteries pumping. Now a twisted corridor.

There's a congress of apostles
& everyone is invited; the thug

to bitter cop cruising the slums. Cut
to the dealer, the suit endlessly scheming.

When the feds come, there's no
body. No gun or knife on the kitchen floor.

No questions on who did it. Cue
McArthur Park, sunlit

& gentrified. Just think about it
add the border crosser in the tenement quarters

all celluloid & noir, a look that says
don't ask. Perhaps it's true. Perhaps

it's the desert. The bougainvillea
in the sand can tell you why.

We step into the air-cooled lobby
the "B" spot of a double-bill movie house

smoke in the air, the rain nocturnal
so dark, enough to get us infected.

There's something of a "B" movie, a snapshot
into someone else's life when you slip on their coats
carry on with their thoughts, maybe the whole life
of a person who lived in these boots. They pull me
like a light that shines from a window on a dark street.
What is it like to enter the other side of that light?
What is it like to sit in the parlor, while gin & lime
waltz in a glass. Is it like an outing to a hotel bar?

Sometimes I just want to find a blue t-shirt that says
Salvadorean Lost in Space, but all they have is this
feathered hat, Chesterfield jacket that ought to be shelved
in the attic. What does it mean for every reed that comes
from a sodden tree to return to its case. What does it take
for the orchestra to go hush. Nothing is left of those days.

ECHO PARK POEM

I've got that Johnny Pacheco
kind of feeling tonight
& I want to drop it
like a 4 x 4 in the middle
of the road, break it down
like it's Africa, 1974.
In Angeleno Heights
from my bungalow window
strung with Christmas lights
I can see in the dark
the buildings, downtown, sick
with their own sweats, monolith
of a mattress & shopping cart
beneath the palm tree.
There's an international agitator
in my kitchen who's got
the blues in his alligator boots
a blathering feeling that matinées
are the best time for b-movies
for the most part film noir.
Everything in my Echo Park
bungalow is an off rhyme.
Not like the oblique Emily
Dickinson, but more like
Antônio Carlos Jobim
Desafinado, Cheo Feliciano
scrolled tight into a bass line

terse, imaginative
& utterly funky. It's true
my flat was a nightclub
in some hole in the wall
in Havana, but this time
everyone gets to keep
their money, carousing
like trains by the turntable
some wrapped in tobacco
leaves, some a bit of rum
to loosen the tongue. Others
philosophizing about home
& whiskey, top shelf. All the shots
are the same & all the shots
are good. I got that
from a little Irish man
outside Dublin. Today
the gentrified streets
of Echo Park are far
from my feet. Now I know
I want my hands resting
over the table the way
Bill Evans hunches
over the piano. All night
I've orbited the moons
of my inheritance
three parts coffee, two parts milk
a pinch of sugar to beat
the devil out of his mind
& easily come up complete.

SPANISH LESSON WITH A HANDFUL OF DIRT

Todos vuelven a la tierra en que nacieron - Ruben Blades

You can always claim your roots
in a country once you bury the dead
or is it your dead will claim you always
once you bury your country. I think
bury the dead & your country roots
will bury you is a variation nailed
& final. If Ruben can return in one song
perhaps I can return in a sentence
maybe the word in Spanish for return
or just *recordar* from the Latin *re-cordis*.
No matter, after my father disappeared
wearing a light shirt & dark colored pants
I started listening to his records, sounds
between the conga & the piano player.
Did you know Ruben reminded everyone
during the Cold War it was too hot
in Central America? I do not understand
this lust of how to kill a man. They broke
my father by the alleyway, something
ghastly, even Dante trembled in his pity.
Did the Bible say don't talk to the dead.
They are many & they want out. I think
my father said it best when he told me

you don't have to teach the dead to talk.
They know what to say. They say spring.
They say summer leaves & a handful of dirt.
They might disappear, go back to wherever
they came from, just when you realize
you're accustomed to their sounds.

BECAUSE THE TREES ARE DISAPPEARING

Early morning, the fog has already covered
the mountains, concealed the little houses

even the lights on the main drag are dumb.
It's cold. Colder than usual, the fog

seems to say, as if at the back of the mind
confusion remains. The fog

can keep us in the dark like that, almost
insensible, the cruel majority to blow off

our coats, to once and for all maintain
its frigid banner reigning all winter long.

Somehow it has locked the gate
severe in its conscience turned

the lights out. Even the neighbor's boy
has begun to laugh it off. Somehow

it has brought flags to the back of trucks
like some fox tail caught on a witch hunt

more isolated, more inaccurate than ever.
No one recognized it, but it came anyway.

COMBUSTIBLE

I don't understand it, this tinder
so difficult to quench
by the minute; cigarette flung

from car to brush
& I am overwhelmed

by the burning smell. The highway
like a long ache all scorched.

Nothing but the clean crack
of leaves, cacti, mountain lion at the door

weather everyone north-faced adores
so I'm told. What else would you expect
from a possum rattling your garbage.

What else would you expect
from shades drawn, & the AC responds
to another call. A crow responds

with a single caw as if he knows
when night arrives sprinklers
will flood the lawn—viridian green.

Still, I am here, the whisper of a thistle

straddled to my backyard, my loused-up
lawn chair meant to be replaced

burnt-out barbecue, my umbrella drink
crashed, radiating like a coiled lightbulb.

THREE SAD STEPS TO HEAVEN

After Philip Larkin

After installing the shelves
in the pantry, mid-December
descending for a smoke
I go out for a steaming shout
of fresh air on the patch
of dead grass. Which is to say
something must be done
about the loneliness it takes
to imagine the dead, which is
a word with a lot of deadweight
for the pallbearer, for dusk light
coming on like a tint of blue
nicked, with no attention
to Mack trucks cussing
like the B-side of a 45.
Something tells me to climb
the plastic tree house, something
tells me I am so near, so far.
Don't confuse your pros & cons.
Here a plane, here a crow locked
on a telephone wire, 7-11 corner
with more scrapyard cars spatting
than the long crawl of ants
I can see from my three sad steps
over the ivy's fence. I, too, shiver

knowing it's in the shaky rooftops
of the Christmas trees, out of
dark mountain throats where the sky
fades like a staircase, but I am
no wolf howling at the moon's pallor.
Inside me is a casket where I prefer
the dead to this cold, muted moon,
this fleck of foam puffing itself wide
like a stare. There's as much darkness
around the Os of the moon as there is
much dirt in a grave. I'd love to hear
you tell me what it's like to see me
propped, what it's like to see me
drift in and out of clouds. Tell me
at least how my absence grounds
you with the pin of a needle. No one
walking the streets is here to see it.

All the dead I'm tired of losing are no longer tufts of wild grass
nor seeds of yellow flowers. I've decided to sit them at the table
flesh & stone, mineral & leaf rot. I've developed a sixth sense for
    this
one you might disregard as dust on your shoulder. It can make
    you
invisible as tame. Most third world people know this. Their
    bodies
descend unseen over the tabletop, astonished by the smell.
Is this why I feel nostalgic, pleading for questions answered?

Why can't I say it again? Everybody else has. I want to sink
    deeper
tierra y agua, rocks & gold bought & bribed, deeper into the
    zopilote
of your song, your outrageous consciousness down like a carcass.
I want to make a name out of your rapture, out of the lights
I plucked out of your sockets. The dead on my chest are still
    healing
but I got over it. Over the headstones, tufts of wild withered hair
it felt real & surreal, how chrysanthemums have begun to take
    shape.

DOUBLE

There used to be a Salvadorean
boy inside this body. And if this
isn't enough he has come back
to tell me it's impossible

to get rid of him, like the year
his father split when he was nine
stranded in the outskirts of some
fictitious town, with nowhere to go

nothing to do, no friends or relatives
to bring him back. And if this
isn't enough his thoughts
walk me back to the year

when I was a wheel. Another
late night talk, & I'm another man
younger, in love with a landscape
I used to know, knows me still

which is to say I'm still here
in the dark, melancholic drunk
on cane vodka & no village drunk.
It is not the cold north

that makes him feel colder
not the wet grass dappled in mud

that makes him stiff. It's my aspiration
to retreat higher & higher

to the mountains, the fact
that I have not listened to a word
he has said that makes him feel
like a lonely song. Has it always

been like this? Most nights
it's quiet. Others the muffled sounds
of a conversation next door. Ours
could be heard upstairs, out there

in my neighbor's ear pressed
to the wall. It's a nocturnal thing
& I wanted so much of this
to be two insomniacs in love

with a hole they can't possibly
fill, but carry nonetheless
like a patron saint to have
when they need a little happiness.

NOTES:

The Roberto Armijo quote which appears in the epigraph of this book comes from *Los parajes de la luna y la sangre,* published by editorial Guayampopo, colección Chilam Balam.

"Beyond Bruegel's Shore" is inspired by the painting *Landscape with the Fall of Icarus* by Pieter the Elder Bruegel.

"El Mozote" is inspired by the Memorial for the massacre at El Mozote in El Salvador. The names were taken at random from the list of the dead in Mark Danner's The Massacre at El Mozote.

"Letters & Numbers" refers to members of Barrio 18, known as the numbers, while MS-13 are known as the letters.

"Saturn's Country" is inspired by Francisco Goya's *Saturn Devours his Children.*

"Variations on Motherwell's *Elegies to the Spanish Republic*" takes names at random from Monumento a la Memoria Y la Verdad, San Salvador, El Salvador.

"Because the Trees are Disappearing"—the title references to *What Kind of Times Are These* by Adrienne Rich.

"Spanish Lesson with a Handful of Dirt" - the Ruben Blades epigraph is from the song "Todos Vuelven" from the album *Buscando America* (1984) on Elektra/Asylum Records.

"Three Sad Steps to Heaven"—the title of the poem is an allusion to Miles Davis's Seven Steps to Heaven and Philip Larkin's poem Sad Steps, which is an allusion to another English poem by Sir Philip Sidney (1554-86), sonnet 31 from Sidney's sonnet sequence, *Astrophel and Stella*. Sidney's poem begins with the line, "With how sad steps, O moon, thou climb'st the skies."

ACKNOWLEDGMENTS:

To the editors and staff of the following publications in which some of these poems or earlier versions first appeared, I extend my sincere thanks for recognizing my voice and acknowledging my work.

Acentos Review, Agni, Atlanta Review, Conjunctions, Colorado Review, Indiana Review, Los Angeles Review of Books, Missouri Review Poem-of the-Week, *Northwest Review, Orion Magazine, Patrik, Pleiades, Prairie Schooner,* Poets.org Poem-A-Day, *Poetry Northwest, Poetry Magazine, Shrewlit Magazine, Tin House,* and *Zócalo Public Square.*

The Academy of American Poets republished "Beyond Bruegel's Shore," "Childhood," "El Mozote," and "Saturn's Country."

"Spanish Love Songs" was republished in the Latino Heritage Cultural Guide 2019, presented by the City of Los Angeles Department of Cultural Affairs. "Las Tías" and "Echo Park Poem" were republished in the Latino Heritage Cultural Guide 2022, presented by the City of Los Angeles Department of Cultural Affairs.

"Advice to a Migrant Collecting Dead Things" appears in *The BreakBeat Poets Volume 4: LatiNext* (Haymarket Books).

"Northern Triangle Dissected" was featured in the Multi-Verse Poetry Podcast hosted by Evangeline Riddiford Graham.

"Echo Park Poem" was featured in the Los Angeles Public Library Poems on Air Podcast by the Los Angeles poet laurate Lynne Thompson.

An earlier version of "Cine Negro" was featured in The Write by Night, a video series on noir poems from Poetry LA hosted by Suzanne Lummis.

"Civil Engineering" was republished in *Patrik* for The Noir Issue, Vol XVIII, No. 4.

Gratitude to Doug Manuel, Joe Millar, and Brian Turner for their comments and encouragement in making this collection possible. Many thanks go to Campbell McGrath, Marjorie Agosin and Rigoberto Gonzalez. Special thanks to Camille T. Dungy, Michael McGriff, Carol Muske-Dukes and Dante Di Stefano for noticing my work. I also want to thank Black Lawrence Press and Fresno State's MFA in creative writing for bringing this collection to life. My gratitude to Mai Der Vang and Diane Goettel for reading and honoring my work. I extend my sincere gratitude to Douglas Kearney for selecting my manuscript for the Philip Levine Prize for Poetry. And of course, thank you Mr. Levine.

My deepest gratitude goes to my lovely and beautiful wife the poet Lory Bedikian for her love, support, and inspiring wisdom. These poems would not be possible without her keen eye.

William Archila is the author of *The Art of Exile* which was awarded the International Latino Book Award, and *The Gravedigger's Archaeology* which received the Letras Latinas/Red Hen Poetry Prize. He was also awarded the 2023 Jack Hazard fellowship. He has been published in *Poetry Magazine, The American Poetry Review, AGNI, Copper Nickle, Colorado Review, The Georgia Review, Kenyon Review, Los Angeles Review of Books, The Missouri Review, Pleiades, Poetry Northwest, Prairie Schooner, Indiana Review, TriQuarterly* and the anthologies *The BreakBeat Poets Vol. 4: LatiNext, Latino Poetry: The Library of America Anthology,* and *The Wandering Song: Central American Writing in the United States.* In 2010, he was named a Debut poet by Poets & Writers. He is a PEN Center USA West Emerging Voices fellow. He is an associate editor of Tía Chucha Press. He lives in Los Angeles, on Tongva land.